THE SFP
LookBook

Mercedes-Benz Fashion Week New York
Fall/Winter 2013 Collections

Jesse Marth

SCHIFFER FASHION PRESS
An imprint of Schiffer Publishing, Ltd.

Other Schiffer Books on Related Subjects:

Emerging Fashion Designers 3, 978-0-7643-4029-1, $39.99

Europe: Rising Fashion Designers 2, 978-0-7643-4545-6, $39.99

Library of Congress Control Number: 2013938812

Type set in Futura X-Bld Italic/Arrus BT Italic

ISBN: 978-0-7643-4570-8
Printed in The United States of America

Published by Schiffer Publishing, Ltd.
4880 Lower Valley Road
Atglen, PA 19310
Phone: (610) 593-1777; Fax: (610) 593-2002
E-mail: Info@schifferbooks.com

For our complete selection of fine books on this and related subjects, please visit our website at www.schifferbooks.com. You may also write for a free catalog.

This book may be purchased from the publisher. Please try your bookstore first.

We are always looking for people to write books on new and related subjects. If you have an idea for a book, please contact us at proposals@schifferbooks.com

Schiffer Publishing's titles are available at special discounts for bulk purchases for sales promotions or premiums. Special editions, including personalized covers, corporate imprints, and excerpts can be created in large quantities for special needs. For more information, contact the publisher.

In Europe, Schiffer books are distributed by
Bushwood Books
6 Marksbury Ave.
Kew Gardens
Surrey TW9 4JF England
Phone: 44 (0) 20 8392 8585; Fax: 44 (0) 20 8392 9876
E-mail: info@bushwoodbooks.co.uk
Website: www.bushwoodbooks.co.uk

CONTENTS

ACKNOWLEDGMENTS

I would like to thank my colleague Douglas Congdon-Martin for getting our team well prepared to cover Mercedes-Benz Fashion Week. His photography from Fashion Week is also featured throughout *The SFP LookBook*.

To IMG Fashion, for executing the well-run series of shows that is Fashion Week, even as the snow started to fall and then accumulate quickly. In particular, I'd like to thank Ashley Simmons for supporting *The SFP LookBook* by answering my many questions.

I would like to thank the many individuals at fashion houses and PR firms who helped provide runway images for those shows we were unable to shoot.

To the other photographers/videographers who covered Mercedes-Benz Fashion Week, thank you for sharing your wisdom and for your camaraderie. Whether you realized it or not, the "in the trenches" support you provided was very valuable.

Finally, I would like to thank my wife, Sally, who is a living, breathing fashion encyclopedia. Through her passion for fashion, I've learned more about fabrics, technique, trends, and designers than any fashion magazine, TV program, or website could ever offer. Thank you.

Schiffer Fashion Press's inaugural LookBook, presents ready-to-wear fashions from the Fall/Winter collections shown at Mercedes-Benz Fashion Week in New York. It is a comprehensive reference for the identification and analysis of trends for the season, including interpretations of theme, color, fabric, pattern, and silhouette, which the designers employed broadly in the looks they sent down the runway.

The SFP LookBook features more than 2,500 looks from the Fall/Winter 2013 collections of 80+ designers, including established labels like Michael Kors, Tadashi Shoji, Monique Lhuillier, Diane Von Furstenberg, Badgley Mischka, and Naeem Khan. Also included are emerging labels, like Bibhu Mohapatra, Alon Livne, and Noon by Noor as well as new lines from Nina Skarra, Second/Layer, and David Hart.

With this broad representation of designers, *The SFP LookBook* exhibits an exciting variety of techniques, materials, styles, and concepts. Captured here are high-end looks for sportswear, menswear, and formalwear, including several red-carpet-worthy designs, that show dark glamour (Reem Acra); deep luxurious jewel tones (Carolina Herrera and Monique Lhullier); intricate beading and design details in golds and silvers (Badgley Mischka, Rafael Cennamo, and Naeem Khan); all-white looks in lace, jersey, and fur (Tadashi Shoji, Hervé Léger by Max Azria, and J Mendel); bold colors in vibrant prints (Mara Hoffman and Anna Sui); structured, armor-like construction (Alon Livne, Falguni and Shane Peacock, and Sasquatchfabrix); sweet and feminine fabrics, colors, and silhouettes (Jenny Packham, Candela, and Tadashi Shoji); colors and themes inspired by New York City (Milly by Michelle Smith and Michael Kors); and looks with roots in the styles of the 1960s and 70s (Anna Sui, Trina Turk, and Diane Von Furstenberg).

Of course the Fall/Winter offerings go well beyond these brief descriptions, which you will soon find out as you further study the thousands of fashions within these pages. Whether you are a designer, stylist, blogger, buyer, or fashionista, I hope that *The SFP LookBook* serves you well as a reference for what these collections have to offer.

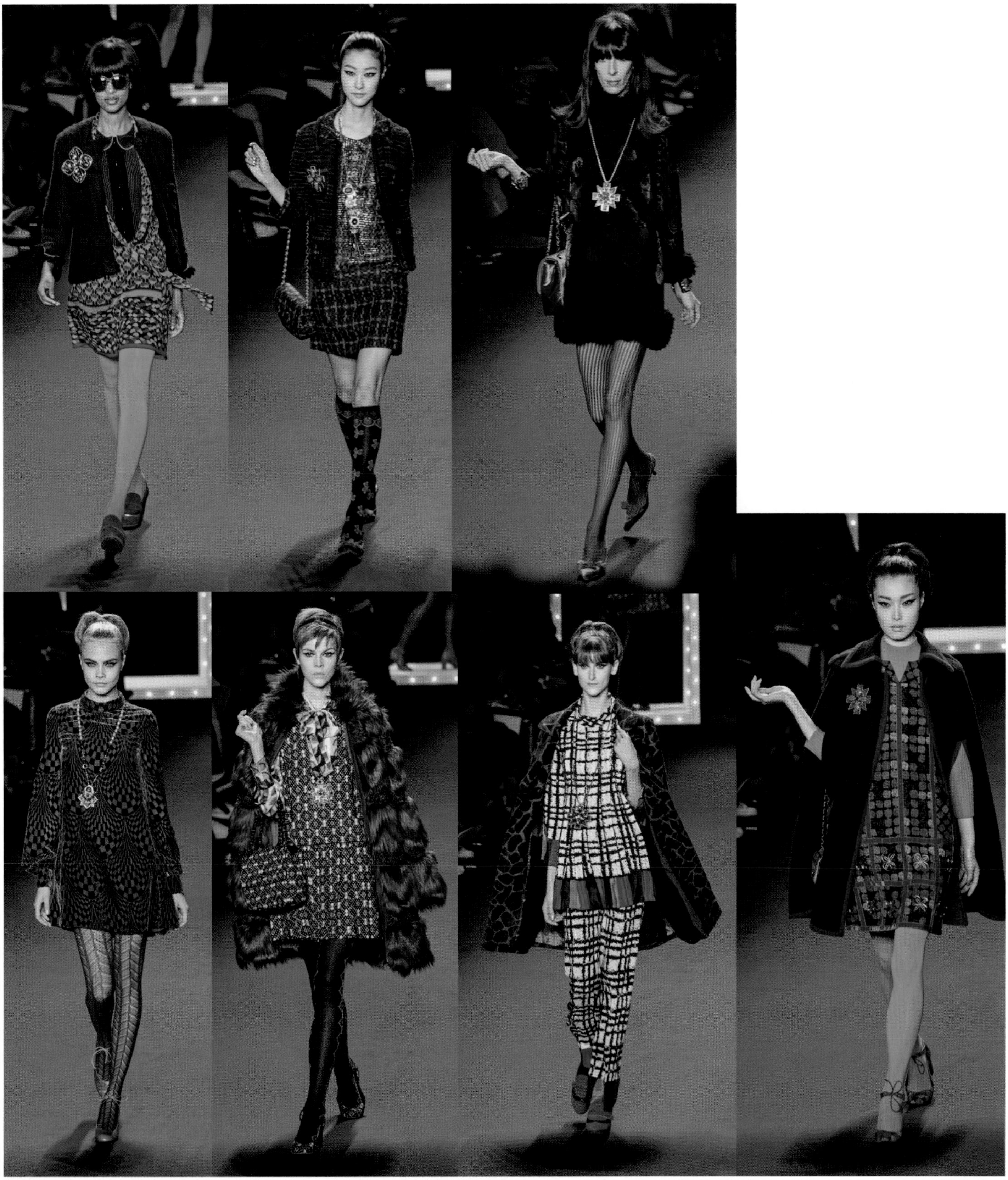

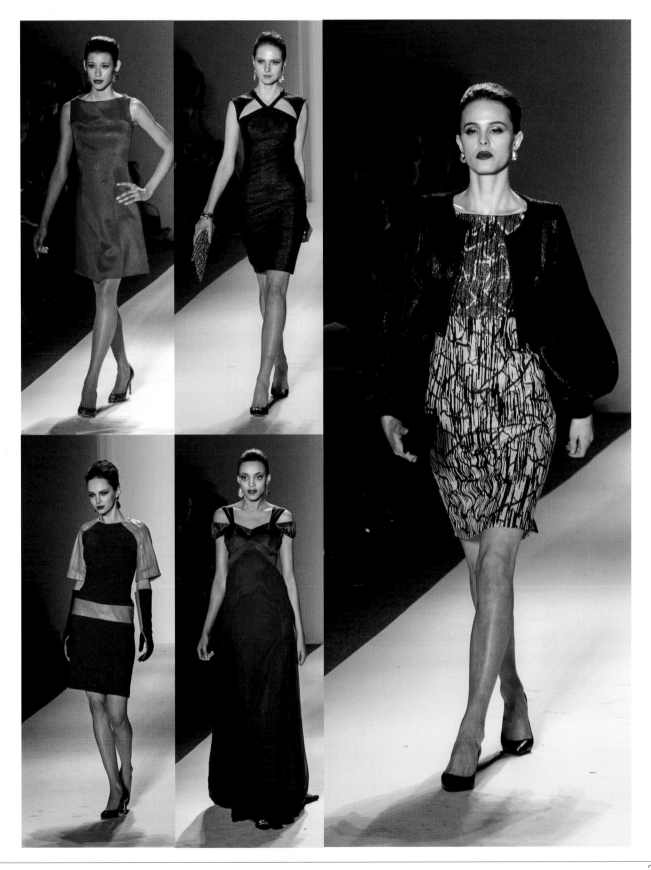

BADGLEY MISCHKA

Mark Badgley & James Mischka, Designers

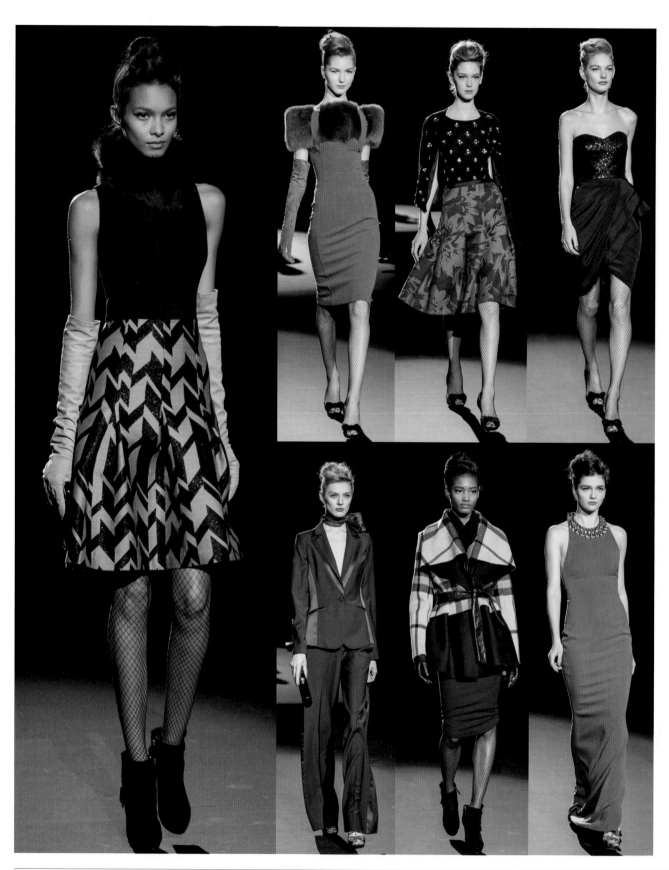

BCBGMAXAZRIA

Max & Lubov Azria, Chief Creative Design Directors

Photos ©Anton Oparin / Shutterstock.com

CONCEPT KOREA: Cres. E Dim.

Hong bum Kim, Designer

CUSTO BARCELONA

Custo Dalmau, Designer

Photos by Tom Concordia, courtesy of Blue Cashew Events

Photos by Tom Concordia, courtesy of Blue Cashew Events

Photos by Tom Concordia, courtesy of Blue Cashew Events

Photos by Tom Concordia, courtesy of Blue Cashew Events

DKNY

Donna Karan, Designer

Photos by Rony Shram, courtesy of Elie Tahari Ltd.

Photos by Rony Shram, courtesy of Elie Tahari Ltd.

Photos by Rony Shram, courtesy of Elie Tahari Ltd.

J. MENDEL

Gilles Mendel, Designer

LACOSTE

Felipe Oliveira Baptista, Designer

Photos courtesy of MM6 by Maison Martin Margiela

Photos courtesy of MM6 by Maison Martin Margiela

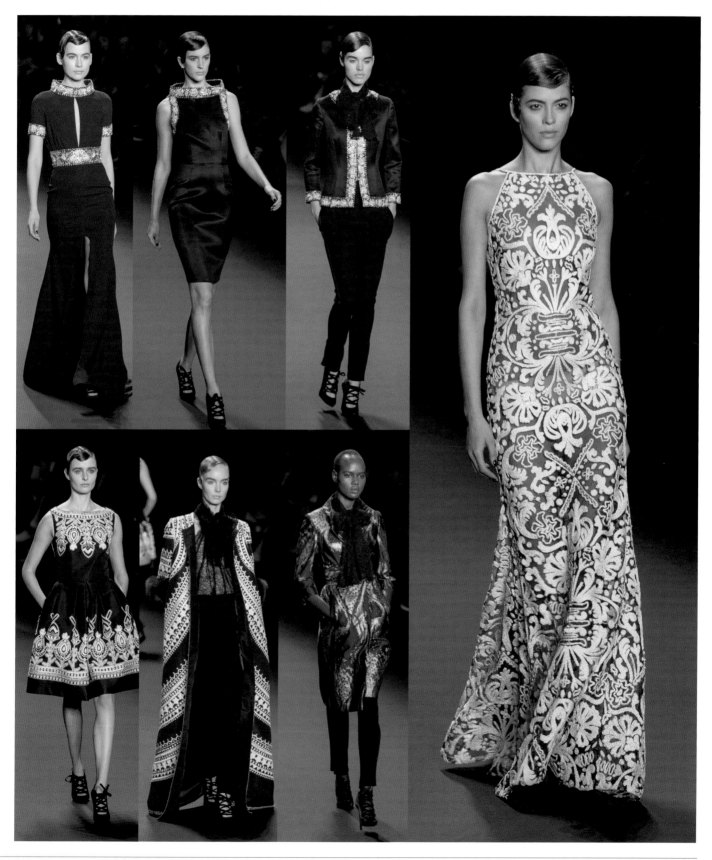

NAUTICA

Chris Cox, Designer

Shaikah Noor Al Khalifa & Shaikah Haya Al Khalifa, Designers

SECOND/LAYER

Second/Layer Team, Designers

Photos by Dan Lecca, courtesy of HL Group

Ready to Write a Book?

We're always seeking authors for a wide variety of topics. This is your opportunity to shine! See our website to view an extensive list of our titles. If this idea appeals to you, we'd love to hear from you. Review our book submission guidelines at our website by clicking on the "Submit a Book Proposal" link. Then email your proposal and ideas to **info@schifferbooks.com** or write to the attention of **Acquisitions** at the address below. You can also call 610-593-1777 to make an appointment to speak with an editor.

◊ Schiffer Publishing
has books covering a wide variety of interests including:

Antiques, Collectibles, & The Arts
Advertising • Automobilia • Black Collectibles • Breweriana • Ceramics • Clocks • Corkscrews • Decoys • Dolls • Fine Art • Folk Art • Furniture • Graphic Art • Holidays • Hunting • Jewelry • Kitchen • Lighting • Leatherwork • Metalware • Native American Crafts • Nautical • Pinball • Quilts • Rugs • Sports • Teddy Bears • Telephones • Textiles • Toys • Video Games • Vintage Fashion • Watches • Writing Instruments and more.

Design, Lifestyle, & D-I-Y
Architecture • Astrology • Counter Culture • Culinary Arts • Erotica • Interior Design • Kitchens and Baths • Landscaping • Numerology • Paranormal • Pin-Ups • Pop Art • Tarot • Tattooing • Textile Design • UFOs • Witchcraft • Basketry • Beads & Jewelry Making • Carving • Furniture Making • Gourds • Home & Garden • Metalwork • Modeling • Pyrography • Sculpture • Textiles • Weaving • Wood Turning • Tools and more.

Military, Aviation, & Automotive History
WWI & WWII Armor/Aviation: German • U.S. • British • Russian • the Jet Age • Unit Biographies and Autobiographies • Edged Weapons • Firearms • Uniforms and more.

Maritime
Seamanship • Navigation • Ship Management • Towing • Transportation • Boats & Boat Building • Medical • Legal and more.

Regional
History • Children's Books • Architecture • Photography • Landscaping • Paranormal • Souvenir • Guidebooks • Cooking and more.

To learn more, go to **www.schifferbooks.com**
Call 610-593-1777, 8:30a.m.-5:30 p.m. EST
or write to 4880 Lower Valley Road
Atglen, PA 19310 USA
and ask for a free catalog(s).

In the UK and Europe contact
Bushwood Books at 44 (0) 20 8392-8585
info@bushwoodbooks.co.uk

Timo Weiland & Alan Eckstein, *Designers*

TIMO WEILAND WOMEN'S

Timo Weiland & Alan Eckstein, Designers

VENEXIANA

Kati Stern, Designer